ANTHOLOGY OF POETRY
BY
YOUNG AMERICANS®

2003 EDITION
VOLUME I

Published by Anthology of Poetry, Inc.

©*Anthology of Poetry by Young Americans*®
2003 Edition
Volume I
All Rights Reserved©

Printed in the United States of America

To submit poems
for consideration in the year 2004 edition of the
Anthology of Poetry by Young Americans®,
send to: poetry@asheboro.com or

        Anthology of Poetry, Inc.
        PO Box 698
        Asheboro, NC 27204-0698

Authors responsible
for originality of poems submitted.

The Anthology of Poetry, Inc.
307 East Salisbury • P.O. Box 698
Asheboro, NC   27204-0698

Paperback ISBN: 1-883931-38-X
Hardback ISBN: 1-883931-37-1

Anthology of Poetry by Young Americans®
is a registered trademark of
Anthology of Poetry, Inc.

While the mathematician is bound by numbers, locked into equations, shackled by formulas set down as unbreakable laws, the heart of an artist is open. While the scientist toils away under the weight of empirical evidence, corralled by a framework of controls, the heart of an artist is free. While the geographer plots his map with layers of lines and legends of reference, he is burdened with the finite, with the unmistakable edges of knowable territories, yet the heart of the artist is boundless. As the historian relates events of the past through indisputable facts, confined in the telling by a definitive start and an ultimate end, the heart of an artist creates.

For fourteen years, the Anthology of Poetry by Young Americans has provided a blank canvas for thousands of young artists to create works of art and share their works with millions across the country. In those fourteen years we have witnessed the open heart at work in love, at work in laugh, and at work in the drama that has moved us through this remarkable, beautiful journey called life.

This fourteenth year adds yet a new dimension to our colorful journey. The artists are open, blossomed, like the earliest spring crocus on that late winter day, when that gasp that you hear is the catch of your breath as you see the color all over again, and for the very first time.

It is with the greatest pleasure that we deliver to you, the blossoms of our children's hearts…

The Editors

LOOK OUT

Sitting deep
Double eyed
Watching your every move
Waiting for midnight's glare
The eagle

Maritza Mestre
Age: 9

THREE EXCUSES FOR HOMEWORK

Number 1
my colossal pig
chomped on it
like it was a juicy
rotten apple
Number 2
my dad ate it
for breakfast
Number 3
my cat
used it as
a litter box
still
I lost recess

Nicholas Robert Marshall

LUV BUG

When I awoke one morning,
A bug was on my head.
I asked, "What are you doing there?"
He looked at me and said...

"I'm here to bring you luck I see,
That is why I'm here.
For if I truly scared you,
I am sorry for that my dear."

"That's quite all right," I replied to him,
"It is no big deal."
"Oh, I'm glad you've forgiven me,
I didn't know how I made you feel."

This bug was odd and very strange,
It was red and black.
It said it was a ladybug,
With spots upon its back.

He said, "Now that I have visited you,
I have to fly away.
I bring good luck to at least
Five children every day."

I asked him why he does this
Because it is very odd.
He said, "It is what I do,
It is like my job."

I opened my window,
With a big fffwwwaaattt!
I said good-bye after
Our short chat.

After my friend left,
I rushed down the stairs.
When I told my parents what had happened,
They gave me that parent glare.

They sent me to my bed,
Thinking I was sick.
I rushed under the covers,
To read my comics.

When I looked out my window,
Guess who it was, just think.
Yes, it was the ladybug,
Giving me a last wink.

Nicole Lamoureux
Age: 11

PASSING JUDGMENT

One thousand rumors
One million lies
Only one tries
To see
What really lies
Inside

Many hurts that come from words,
That simply are not true
And when you try to prove them wrong
They simply overlook you

They've placed a wall of He said/She said
'Round your face and name
They've given you a label
They've given you a place
Try as you might
This is something you can't change,
And after all these rumors you're never quite the same

Judge me
Not by what you think you see,
Nor by what you've heard
YOU! Come and see what you might find
In entering my world

Kristyn E. Lattanzi
Age: 14

I DREAM

After a long day in the fields; when the sun sets
and your ears perk up for the sound of quitting time,
I lay my head and count my blessings.
I pray the Lord my soul to keep.
I daze and travel to the world of dreams, far faraway.
I pass through mist and see, a lamb
next to a flowing spring in the middle of all pastures.
I feel drawn to the stillness of the water
and the greenness of the pastures.
As I pass the lamb in what seems paradise,
I enter a valley.
I feel the presence of chains, whips, sweat, heat,
starvation, sickness and even death.
The valley has a shadow of despair
that which I shudder at the mere sight.
I pick up my pace, hoping that this torment will end.
As the valley is surrounded by mist
I see a table filled with food of great delicacy.
I feel the presence of the same emotion
as I had in the pasture; but I feel shielded, protected,
as if none of my enemies can ever harm me.
I look up towards the heavens
and see a great massive castle.
And a great king on a throne of sun drops
and moonbeams.
His voice rolls like the deepness of thunder.
I fear but strain to hear what he has to say.
I awake at the beginning of a brand-new day.

Christina Helen Smith
Age: 13

MOTHER NATURE

Oh, beautiful, sweet, Mother Nature.
Has the sun, the flowers, and the grass.
The clouds in the sky and the gorgeous butterflies
fluttering their wings all day long.
The birds singing a delightful song.
Oh how I long to be outside with Mother Nature.

Holly Arel
Age: 10

I do a lap around the rink
I do a figure eight
I move on to one of my favorites
the spins
I am relaxed when I skate
like my problems went down the drain
When I do a jump
I'm soaring above the rink
I feel cold when I fall
and my fingertips freeze
I do a graceful waltz jump
I do it again from backward crossovers
into a landing position
then I jump
I leave the rink
I'm tired
I can't wait to come back next time

Laura M. Figueroa

LIGHTS

We use lights to
   Read a book
We use lights to
   Do our homework
We use lights to
   Paint and draw
We use lights to
   Play a game
We use lights to
   Use the computer
We use lights to
   Watch TV
We use lights to
   Eat our food
We use lights to
   Decorate
We use lights to
   Drive our cars
We use lights to
   Look at pictures
We use lights for EVERYTHING

Caitlin Reed
Age: 11

DISNEY CHARACTERS

Mickey has a girlfriend named Minnie.
She has a friend named Pooh
But everyone calls him Winnie the Pooh.

Donald has three nephews, Huey, Duey, and Louie.
Maybe they should have another brother named Truey.

Mickey has a dog
His name is Pluto.
I wonder where he was born
Maybe it was on Pluto.

Goofy has a car.
He's the only person that can drive the highway loop.
You can see him do that on Goof Troop.

Something that rhymes with bend is lend.
I know that you know that this is the end!

Jacob Hernandez
Age: 10

It leaps in the sun
she pauses and looks at me
then the deer moves on.

Courtney Milne

THANKSGIVING

Thanksgiving is my favorite holiday.
It makes me feel special in everyway.

On Thanksgiving we have a lot to eat.
Turkey, mashed potatoes, and pie that tastes sweet.

I am thankful for my family, they love me dearly.
That's why I love Thanksgiving
And I hope it keeps on yearly.

Jennifer Korona
Age: 10

BUGS

Bugs are crawly.
Bugs are creepy.
Bugs are sometimes very sleepy!
Bugs are slick
And can be quick.
Some are cool,
And sometimes drool!
Some have shells,
But none have bells.
Some make you scratch,
Others you want to catch.
Bugs can be both good and bad.
Some make you happy and some make you sad!

Conor Olejarz

MY PARENTS

Who taught me how to walk,
And taught me how to talk?
  My father

Who taught me how to pray,
And to listen in God's special ways?
  My mother

Who is the one who took me to the game,
And the one who calls me special names?
  My father

Who is the one who bought me a cat,
And the one who hated my very old rat?
  My mother

Who was the one who taught me to think,
And the one who hates the color pink?
  My father

Patrick Strepka
Age: 10

THE SUNSET

Looking outside I see the sun glow into my eyes,
It is so beautiful how it sets
With the red, pink, purple, and blue.
Sometimes I wonder where it comes from,
Then I look at the sunset
And see God's beautiful gift to us.

Robert Doyle
Age: 11

MY FAMILY

My name is Dan.
My last name is Poe.
My favorite game is Clue, you know.

My brother's name is Matt.
He likes to ride his bike a lot,
But he doesn't like to get a shot.

My mother's name is Maryann.
She likes to read lots of books
And she's the one who always cooks.

My dad's name is Glenn.
He works on the kitchen almost every day.
He never really has time to play.

Daniel Poe

SNOW

Falling from the sky above,
   landing like a song sweet dove.
Putting love in hearts of many,
   something that brings joy to everyone all around.
Swirling from the mountaintops,
   making a lot of sudden drops.

Catherine Leonard
Age: 11

AFRAID

Afraid of the dark,
Afraid of the storm,
I'm so frightened.

Afraid of the Boogie Monster
Under my bed,
Afraid of the Wicked Witch of the West,
Why am I so scared?

Afraid of the noise outside my window,
Afraid of the evil laugh when the lights go off,
But, this is just all just my IMAGINATION.
I think!

Taylor McInerney

JUST MY LUCK

Just my luck,
  My brother is
In a bad mood
  And is talking
To a talking dog
  Very bad attitude.

Meaghan Knightly
Age: 10

GREEN

Green is the color of the grass.
Green is the color of the leaves.
Green is the color of the board.
Green is the color of the books I have.
Green is the color of the car.
Green is the color of the planners.
Green is the color of the backpack of mine.
Green is the color of the Christmas tree.
Green is the color of the cactus.
Green is the color of the house.
Green is the color of the bushes.
Green is the color of the flowers' leaves.
Green is the color of the spelling notebook of mine.

Tevin Jimenez

A DOE

Once I saw a doe,
in the bright, white snow.

She was near a tree,
staring back at me.

At the flick of her tail,
she ran down the trail.

And that was the end
of the doe for me.

Alyssa Lempart
Age: 9

THANKSGIVING AGAIN

1620 the Pilgrims came.
1621 the first Thanksgiving feast started.
Squanto first taught them to plant corn.
They made lots of food.
There was turkey, stuffing, bread, pie, potatoes and corn.
There was friends, family, and fun,
Bells, music, and more.
Love, and happiness,
It ended then the years later it still continues.

Ryan J. Chlosta

TODAY, BEFORE TOMORROW

Today before tomorrow
Means we don't know
The future

Today means we know
Tomorrow means we
Don't know

Tomorrow comes and goes
Now we know

Kimberly Estey
Age: 10

WILD BOY

Screaming with joy
Climbing with joy
Chomping with joy
Tossing with joy

A great big grinful of laughter

A baby boy
My brother

Noam Zilberstein

THANKFUL

I am thankful for having a cat
Also thankful for a hat
And thankful for my baby brother, Stanley
And I guess my family

Samantha Anderson
Age: 10

MY DOG

I love my dog,
He likes to run and play,
He hogs his ball,
So we can't play.

When we come in from playing,
He takes a nap,
When he wakes up he wants to run again.

He eats all day,
When he's not playing.

He begs and whines,
When he doesn't get his way.

But, I still love my dog.

Breeanna Clarke

YOU CAN'T SCARE ME!

I bet you can't scare me
it's just not true,
I've been on Superman
and the Drop of Doom.

You can't scare me
I'm so tough,
I've been in an army tank
and lots of other stuff.

I'm sure you can't scare me
I'm just too brave,
I've swam near stingrays
and been in a bear cave.

Nobody can scare me
not even my friend Mark,
I'm not afraid of anything
except for the dark!

Stephanie Collins
Age: 9

GREEN

Green is the main color of St. Patrick's Day.
Green is the color of a clover
Also, the color of a crayon.
Green is the color of grass.
Green is the color of a Christmas tree.
A frog is the color green
A stem of a flower, too.
Moss on a rock is the color green.
There are many, many
Things in the world
That are green.

Jennifer Cardinal
Age: 9

SCHOOL

School is cool
Cooler than a pool
School is where you do some math
You might even write a paragraph
School is where you are reading
At music you will start singing
School is where you do social studies
You might even do it with some buddies
After a year of education
You deserve a celebration

Dakota Prive

MY TWO HAMSTERS

I have two little hamsters.
They like to play all day.
They spin and eat.
And like to sleep.
Did I tell you they're mine?

I have two little hamsters.
They're only one month old.
Squeaky's black and white.
Elmo's white and tan.
They fight all day.
And play all night.
But! I'm glad they're mine.

Taylor Ross
Age: 10

SOCCER

Soccer is cool,
It's better than school.
Soccer is fun,
If you like to run.
Soccer is better than a boring book report,
Soccer is my second favorite sport.

Caitlin Charette

THE DAY, THE MONTH, THE YEAR

That day I thought I'd die.
Once so tall, now nothing.
Nothing at all.
Once so alive, now dead
The month 9, the day 11
The year, 2001.

Sean Gregory

MY BAD DAY

In the morning it was pouring.
  Dad is mad he is roaring.
Breakfast is not made.
  My allowance I've not been paid.
My school clothes are all wrinkled.
  All my papers are now crinkled.
My backpack weighs a ton.
  Walking to school isn't going to be fun.
The sticks on the sidewalk made me trip.
  The ice on the ground made me slip.
Homework is not done.
  My bad day has just begun.

Bridget A. Peery
Age: 10

MONKEYS

Monkeys, monkeys everywhere!
Swinging crazy in the air.
Can't they sit there in a chair
And brush and comb their own hair?
Monkeys, monkeys everywhere!
(I think they're in my own hair!)

Drew Curry

Itchy itchy chickenpox
  scratching all day long.
Itchy itchy chickenpox
  my brother says ha ha.
Itchy itchy chickenpox
  spending all day at home.
Itchy itchy chickenpox
  where is that comb.
Itchy itchy chickenpox
  now they are all gone.
Itchy itchy chickenpox
  now my brother has some.
Itchy itchy chickenpox
  don't come to our house!

Katelyn Kurpaska

WHEN I JUMP IN THE LEAVES

In the fall
the leaves
come down
from
top
to
bottom
like rain.
I rake them
into
big, fat piles
and jump right in!
I hear
Crunch, Crunch.
And when I feel the wind
on me
I fall
right down
into
the pile
of leaves.

Chad Lapinski
Age: 8

FALL

Fall, fall, fall.
Fall is great.

Leaves change
to different bright colors.
Leaves
drip
out of the trees,
back and forth,
like a feather.

Pumpkin time.
Let's pick pumpkins.
Big light orange pumpkins
as bright as the sun
or the moon.
Little brown stems
like fat little beads.

Fall, fall, fall.
Fall is great!

Evan Haas
Age: 8

WHO IS YOUR FRIEND?

Friend, friend.
Who is your friend?
My, my.
My friend, you say?

Who is your friend,
I say?
Is your friend black?
No.
Is your friend red?
No.
Is your friend tan?
Yes!

It is a she.
Is her name Maya?
Yes.
How do you know?
Well, well.
She is my friend.
Oh.

Who is your friend?
It's a
secret.

Laurel B. King
Age: 8

24

THINGS I LIKE

I like the sky,
baby blue like my eyes.
I like the grass,
dark green like a leaf.
I like butterflies,
flying like birds.
They land on your hand
and they tickle you
with their antennae.
I like caterpillars,
soft like a feather
across your hand.

Cherylynn Laveck
Age: 7

MY CAT

Black, white, brown.
Green eyes
glow in the dark.
She sounds like
a copy machine
when she purrs.
She plays on a chair
with her mouse.

Jenna Blair

HALLOWEEN

Walking on the road.
Jack-o'-lanterns
mean, happy, sad faces.

Cats on a fence
jump like a bunny,
scaring me.

Candy that looks real
at home
waiting for me.

Adam Christopher
Age: 7

CHRISTMAS

Christmas is fun.

Yu-Gi-Oh cards.
You get lots and lots of presents.
You decorate your Christmas tree.
It has breakable things that sing.
When you are sleeping at night
Santa Claus brings presents.

Christmas is fun.

Tommy Dudkiewicz

SUMMER

When the sun shines out
It's nice and bright,
I like to go outside and play
With the shining above my head,
The birds flying everywhere,
I like to catch butterflies,
I like to go swimming,
And best of all I love to go on vacation.

Kathryn Daponte
Age: 9

MY DOG

My dog jumps
like a football player
to catch a Frisbee.
His leg
flings out.
When he barks
it sounds like
a plane taking off.
He catches
the Frisbee
high in the air.
I say,
"Good dog!"

Samantha Corbeil

BOOKS

Rectangular prism shape
They take you anywhere!
Countries, regions, times, people, animals

Different titles, different genres
They take you anywhere!
Mystery, historical, fantasy, adventure

Books are great!
No matter what!

Alex Randall
Age: 9

I MADE UP

I made up nonsense
I made up stop it
I made up go to your room
I made up quiet
I made up stay in for recess
I made up nuisance
I made up go away
I made up leave me alone please
I made up all those words

Kristina Collins

FROGS

Hop, hop anywhere on a lily pad.
In a pond on dry land frogs go hopping mad.
But when you catch them they soon die.
It's frogs that croak when they hop high.

Brett Nowlan
Age: 9

THE OLYMPIC DREAM

The Olympic dream is about to come true,
Here in Greece, the sky is blue,
From the great soaring athletes,
With rapid heartbeats,
To the remarkable Opening Ceremony,
With gold medals shiny,
The Olympic dream is about to come true.

The runners are going to run,
The audience is having loads of fun,
Soccer teams are ready to win,
Athletes to be shown on television,
The Olympic dream is about to come true.

THE OLYMPIC DREAM IS ABOUT TO COME
TRUE!!

Max Lu

LEAVES

I jump
I play
In the red,
      orange,
       yellow,
        green,
          and brown leaves that fell from the trees,
I rake
I pile
The leaves up over and over again.

I JUMP

Margaret Prentice
Age: 9

9-11-2001

The day of 9-11 was the death of many Americans
And the Twin Towers,
American hearts break with tears,
Twin Towers fell,
We have to face our fears,
Now celebrations with family are gone,
Sky is dark,
Firefighters never forget 9-11
And the Americans that have died.

Ryan Daley

ALL ALONE

One dark spring night I was all alone
Sitting, staring I was all alone
No one but me I was all alone
I heard something when I was all alone
When I woke I heard no more
It was a dream when I was all alone

Ashley Madison
Age: 10

I AM

I am a daughter,
I am a student,
I am a cousin,
I am a niece,
I am an animal owner,
I am a cat lover,
I am a friend,
I am a neighbor,
I am a gymnast,
I am a dancer,

I am anything!

And that's what I am!

Grace Brown

SILENT DREAMS

The fantasies are sworn to be of reality
As they walk all over me,
With their empty souls and discreet movement
They are nothing more than figments of my imagination
Yet popular in the threshold of one's dreams
The blood of the fantasies is washing over the ruins,
Burying them in cemeteries of the naked truth
And the fragments are brewin' up a storm,
Blowin' over the coasts
It scurries over the bend
And chases itself into the endless wood
And collapses into hot, silvery liquid
Until the foam rises and pours over my mind's edges
Smudging the autumn sky
With fingertips dipped in soft gray paint
And now it can only be time
Before God hears my sentimental wishes
Casting a forbidden spell upon such unrealistic fantasies
Some may say my wishes are nothing more than clichés
But do you know what I say?
I say nothing...
Just observe the countless seconds remaining in silence

Meaghan A. Quinn
Age: 13

SOUNDS OF BASKETBALL

Dribble, Dribble,
   Bounce, Bounce,
Swish through the hoop,
   A slapping noise
Of a personal foul,
Quick, squeaky sneakers running,
   The snap of a pass
      Hitting hands,
Again, Dribble, Dribble,
   Swish!

Patrick Dickert
Age: 7

THANKSGIVING

Thanksgiving day is a time for thanks.
It's a time for love.
It's a time of get together,
but above all of that is God.
On that day of thanks we call Thanksgiving,
we thank Him for all we have --
family, love, a home, clothing, food, friends,
and His love for us.
So don't forget to thank Him for what you have.

Jakob Labonte

FRIENDSHIP

Friendship reminds me of a dove,
With lots of love,
Which I will always put above,
It reminds me of truth, and care,
Like I can hug it like a bear,
Just remember, a true friend is always there.

Sasha M. Delgado
Age: 11

I'M AFRAID

I'm afraid,
I'm alone,
I'm in a dark room,
There's a monster in my closet,
There's a google in my wallet,
There's a meek beneath my bed,
And soon I will be dead!
I rush under my covers,
And I see two fuzzy slovers!
I sprint out of my room,
And I see a scary gloom,
Now I'm seeing red,
But it's all inside my head,
When I'm afraid.

Brett Von Flatern

MY STAR-NET

I made a net to reach the sky,
It was eight miles high;
But it won't reach the stars, I don't know why;

I held it straight and tall, I reached out,
and I missed.
I kept trying; I think my net was too short.

I tried one last time. I didn't miss,
I caught something, but it wasn't a star --
It was a car. Uh-oh, got to go!!

Jessica Cygan
Age: 11

I AM THE CAT

I am the cat
Who walks upon the path
Of furious rats and mice
I am the cat
That prowls all day
That prowls all night
Until I make my choice
I am the cat
Who walks upon the path

Stephanie Vlohiotis

THANKSGIVING FOOD

It is Thanksgiving time
The brownies would be all mine
For the turkey,
I was first in line.
It was one of my best meals,
Because my favorite foods were combined.

Michael Anthony Lebiedz
Age: 11

MORNING

The morning sun
So much fun

I love the colors
Around the morning sun
Sometimes red
Sometimes gold

I fold my hands to pray
To God

That I will always see lots of colors
With the morning sun

Alexander J. Malanowski

ALONE

Hey you! Yes, you!
In the blue overalls and the long-sleeve shirt.
Do you know?
Have you heard?
In this small little corridor,
That you are all alone, alone,
All alone.

Sara Davis
Age: 10

FALL NIGHT

The fire roars in smoky clouds
and warms up all the room.

A loon flies above the house
in front of the golden moon.

Stars twinkle silver light
and brighten up the dark cold night.

Hours pass the morn's begun
the sky gets lit by the golden sun.

Melissa Edberg

THE GRAY BLOB NAMED JAY

Once upon a time,
In a land of all good things,
Lived a bunch of happy blobs
Who knew no evil thing.

One day one blob named Jay
Wanted to understand
The cultures of others,
So he traveled to a foreign land.

He saw many evil sights
Which made him very sad.
He had never seen these things before
And now knew what was bad.

But soon Jay got curious.
He wanted to know more.
So he went back to those places
Where he had seen the evil before.

Soon Jay knew how to push and shove
And how to yell and curse,
And now it seemed his perfect nature
Had taken a turn for the worse.

But Jay had a good time anyway,
And as soon as he was home
All his friends wanted to know
What he did when he was gone.

So he told his friends everything
(Except what he had learned)
And all his friends were amazed
At what they just heard.

But then one day when Jay was walking
And someone got in his course
He yelled and screamed at the blob
And then Jay punched and cursed.

The other blob was horrified
And quickly ran away.
He told all his other friends
To stay away from Jay.

And soon the whole blob community
Was too afraid to go near
And all poor Jay could do
Was shed some blobby tears.

So he went to the wise blob's house
And queried what was wrong.
He wanted to know why he had been
Ignored for so long.
The old blob took pity on Jay
And said with a tiny chortle
That he would solve his problems
By teaching Jay this moral:

"So if you do not want to go on
Feeling quite so blue
Do unto others
As you would want them to do to you."

Veronika LaRocque

MAYWAY THE GIRL

Once there was a girl named Mayway,
She always had ten minutes of leeway.
She would always have time
To make up the wrong,
But she never got so far.
She thought she should have things her way,
So friends and families tried talking to her
And so they found out that she was Miss Understood.
People then understood that you can't
Make others do things the same way,
You should expect them to have different ways.
Mayway, then learned that she isn't always
Going to have leeway in her life.
Now she talks to everyone
And then she found out that, that was how
She got her name Mayway,
Because she always had to have things her way.

Lorena Avendano

CRITTERS!

Spooky critters everywhere,
Up from the ground and down from the air.
Mummies, bats, witches too,
And a friendly ghost just saying, "BOO!"
Full moon and autumn air,
Just might give you a little scare.
All together it's a wonderful sight,
Just beware of them on Halloween night!

Anna and Ellen Hutchinson
Age: 12

SOMETIMES

Sometimes there's sun.
Sometimes there're flowers.
Sometimes there're heroes with super powers.

Sometimes there're stars.
Sometimes there're bats.
Sometimes there're big ugly rats.

Sometimes there're tea leaves in the teapot.

That all may be true or at least what I thought.

Steven Talbot

DANCING

I enjoy dancing.
The music has a good beat.
There are pretty shoes.
There are beautiful costumes.
I like twirling and leaping.

Katie Ritchie
Age: 10

VETERANS: OUR STAR-SPANGLED HEROES

With fear upon their faces, and sadness in their eyes,
Men and women are forced to leave their families,
their futures full of surprise.

Victorious they may rise, or sunken they may fall,
Looking back the Veterans remember,
how it began with a single phone call.

We praise them for their willingness to fight,
And honor their courage, day and night.

So as we salute the flag each morning,
We remember and make a tribute to our Veterans,
our Star-Spangled Heroes.

The men and women of the red, white, and blue.

Rebecca Lynn DeSanti

THANKSGIVING DAY

It's Thanksgiving!
The kitchen smells good.
They're making pumpkin pie and turkey.
I love being with my family and friends.
Thanksgiving day!

Amanda Patterson
Age: 10

THANKSGIVING

It's Thanksgiving
the sound of beautiful music
the smell of the feast
the sight of family coming together on Thanksgiving.
Saying grace for all that we have
smelling beautiful candles
seeing the great feast.
Smell a wonderful fire burning
the sight of a warm living room
and listen to a story.
Hear the fire crackling
oh, what a wonderful sight to see
and feel its warm tender glow
let it warm you and keep you snug all through the night.
Don't be unthankful be thankful
of all that you have and that's happened.

Sarah Jayne Cortes

THANKSGIVING DAY

Thanksgiving day was here,
Sounded like my mom was near.
We always celebrate the Pilgrims' and the Indians' feast.
My mom looked like she made a roast beef.
We are thankful for our family.

Nikos Joseph Calkins
Age: 11

THE SMELL

There is something in the air
That I know it's time for winter.
There's something everywhere
That tells you it's time for winter.
The frost on the ground,
The chill in the air,
The kids playing everywhere.
Even though it's cold outside,
The kids are playing everywhere.
They run around,
They shout and scream.
They know it's winter before us.
Before you, before anyone,
Not you or you or you!

Courtney Elizabeth Kazierad

44

MY FRIENDS

My friends are pals to me,
We play soccer and even some rugby,
Hanging with my friends is so much fun,
As we play football in the sun,
My friends are the best,
They are everything to me even pests.

Ryan Shewchuk
Age: 12

THE SEASON OF FALL

Trees are emptying
their branches.
Leaves are changing colors
like sunsets.
The ground is turning
icy cold.
My legs are moving
as fast as a bunny
running from predators.
My stomach is steaming
like an oven.
Pumpkin pie,
Pumpkin pie!
It is fall!

Kierstin Gallo

I don't think of him as gone away
his journey's just begun
life holds so many facets,
this earth is only one.
I think of him as resting
from the sorrows and the tears
in a place of warmth and comfort
where there are no days and years.
I think how he must be wishing
that we could know today
how (wishing) (how)
nothing but our sadness
really pass us by.
And I think of him as living
in the hearts of those he touched
for nothing loved (loved) (loved) (love) is ever lost
and he was loved so much.
Now you are gone away
but the sadness is inside my heart.
I try to hold my tears
but my sadness comes out
and I can't hold it in,
because I love you without a doubt.

Tamari J. Martinez
Age: 11

HALLOWEEN CHILDREN

Halloween
is a day
when lots of children
go trick-or-treating
to get
lots of candy.

Halloween
is a day
when lots of children
dress up
and go for the fun of it.

Halloween
is a time
to get a little
spooked up
for once.

Alex Nielsen

WITHOUT

Without the sun
There would be no moon

Without the tracks
There would be no train

Without the clouds
There would be no rain

Without a dove
There would be no love

All this shows what the world means
Even down to the little greens

Let us take care of our things
Down to our diamond rings

And remember and cherish
                    Everything

Ashley Arpino
Age: 13

THE LIGHTS

Last night I saw this light.
It was so bright that it blinded my eyes.
I tried to look again, but it got harder
and harder to look at the light.
The next night I saw the light again,
but this time the light got closer and closer.
I closed my eyes to get the picture out of my mind,
but when I opened my eyes there it was,
my Guardian Angel watching over me.

Eric Joshua Segundo

WONDERING THE OPTIONS

I walk alone by myself,
wondering what I will put on my shelf?
Books, birds, flowers so nice,
maybe I'll have a statue of ice?
I still hope and wonder,
beyond the younger,
believing it's true,
the color of blue.
I walk alone by myself,
still wondering what I will put on my shelf.

Melissa Rimondi

JOY

Everybody has some joy
we might not show it
in the same way
but we all have joy
Joy

Katrina Sanchez
Age: 10

SAILING ON THE DEEP BLUE SEA

Sailing on the deep blue sea
With my grandpa and me

Sailing on the deep blue sea
With all the fish beneath me

Sailing on the deep blue sea
Watching all the leaves fall from the trees
On an autumn day as we drift away

As we crash over the waves
We sail through the summer haze

Out on the deep blue sea
Are the best times for my grandpa and me.

Ashley Callahan

I AM YOUR CHILD

I am whom you love
to hold tight
and never let go.
I am your fire
to keep you happy and warm
to bring you a warm hug.

I am you.
You look at me and see yourself.
You look and see me.

I am your star.
You are the moon
watching over me.
I am everything you wish for.
I learn from you
and watch what you do.

I am your dream.
In your dreams you see me
and love me even more.

You are my friend.
Someone I can talk to
and share with all my thoughts and dreams
I am your child.

Megan Leahan
Age: 14

SOCCER

I know I'm only ten years old
My love for soccer will never grow old

My happiness is at center field
Though that defense is like a shield
I get the ball and do not yield

I bring the ball to the net
I hope a goal is what I get

As I once was told it's better
To be strong and bold
As I keep my head up high
For my love of soccer I can't deny

I know I'm young but when I get old
I hope I hold a medal of gold

Cadie Trombley
Age: 10

BABY SISTER

Like the meadow by the sea
When I look at thee I see beauty
Baby sister how sweet you are
Like soft shadows whispering afar

Your tender voice and merry laughter
Keep me going farther
100 miles, 1,000 miles a day
Could never keep me away

Little "Hi's" with those lovely eyes
Bring me so many smiles
Without you I am incomplete
Just like the shepherd who lost his sheep

When you hide because you're shy
You make my eyes fill with tears -- I cry
The greatest gift I have ever gotten
Will never be forgotten.

Victoria Gosine
Age: 14

The skies are blue,
I know you
You know me
The skies are blue.

The sun is yellow and bright,
You are my "bestest" friend.
I love my teacher,
I love my family,
I love the way the leaves fall,
I love the way pretty flowers bloom.

Kadence Marie Verge
Age: 6

HORSES

The horses run
like the breeze
They gather around
meadows and trees
They like to play
and like to feed
And they like hay
and eat some seeds

Brianne Jones

GRANDMA

My grandma, she is the best
She may even be better than all the rest
She will swim, hike and canoe
She loves nature and outdoors too!

Even though she works at home
With her scissors and her comb
She'll find time to be at the glen for a few
She loves nature and outdoors too!

While she watches her ten grandkids for the day
As they eat, sleep, and play
She'd bring all of us to the parks and zoos
She loves nature and outdoors too!

You can tell she loves nature very much
Because she started the "Save the Glen" bunch
If everyone only knew
How much, she loves nature and outdoors too!

Amanda Bresett
Age: 13

LIFE

Your life has four seasons --
Spring
When light breezes kiss the earth,
When tiny rosebuds come out from hiding,
When snow melts in tiny pools that run down to the lake,
When salmon swim to their native breeding grounds,
Then you get summer

Summer is when rains fall,
When heat waves come,
When hurricanes drown the earth in waves
of water and sorrow,
Then it is autumn

Autumn is when leaves fall softly from the maples,
When acorns land hard on the ground,
When squirrels cry chi-chi-chitter and the owl goes hoot;
Then it is winter

Winter is when it snows,
Jack Frost comes out of hiding, when we go skiing
Then the great circle of seasons continues
as your life passes by
You see lakes olive green to midnight blue to black
You see green frogs and purple cows
as your life passes by
Big events happen like 9/11
You come in tune to God as your life passes by
Friendships come and go
You meet new teachers, your heart breaks and heals,
You see animals as your life passes by,
...and then you die
That's life.

Moira Anne Wentworth
Age: 11

FOREVER

Friends forever
That's what we'll be
Friends forever
You and me
Memories and good times show
The fact that we will always know
What it is to be a Friend
And that this will never end
As we grow and change our views
We'll stay together through and through
We'll teach each other our new ways
And make sure they'll always stay
When bad times come we'll stick together
Never leaving each forever
Telling everyone we're true Friends
And knowing it will never end
Showing what it means to be
Friends forever you and me

Caitlin Ward

DAD

His name is Rick,
and he's never sick,
he has a black cat
and she is very fat,
but he will always be my dad.

Metallica is his favorite band,
although he hates to walk in the sand,
we all like to run
and I'm his only son,
but he will always be my dad.

He drives a Chevy,
and is not heavy,
he is over thirty,
but he is not dirty,
but he will always be my dad.

He is married to Pat,
but she's not fat.
My dad is funny,
and he likes bunnies,
but he will always be my dad.

My dad always breaks the dish,
but he always catches the fish,
he was in the Navy,
and his best friend is Davy,
but he will always be my dad.

Richard J. Martin
Age: 13

MY STEPMOM

My stepmom is beautiful with her bright blue eyes,
Short dirty blonde hair,
She likes to share.
Also likes to work, helps me with my homework.
Seems like a mother to me.

Works many hours,
Likes to plant flowers.
Also very glad,
Never too sad.
Seems like a mother to me.

Sometimes likes to cook,
When she goes shopping, she likes to look.
Sometimes likes to clean,
Always using the washing machine.
Seems like a mother to me.

Hates when she has to clean the house,
I love her very much,
Has a nice smile,
Always has some sort of style.
Likes to take care of me,
Seems like a mother to me.

Stephanie Carpenter
Age: 13

MY GRANDPA, OLD AND WISE

He may be crippled but at least he tries,
I once heard he wakes up hoping to die.
I remember all those days we had so much fun,
All he wants now is to run.
My grandpa, old and wise.

He looks like a cowboy that rode his horse too long,
Was good at sports 'til something went wrong.
He hurt his knees, that was his problem,
Joined the police and walked less often.
My grandpa, old and wise.

Then he retired, his daughter had me,
Let's not forget what he did to his knees.
Now he's older and so am I,
He's had an operation and is happy to see me,
The first operation was on his right knee.
My grandpa, old and wise.

He looks much better and has only one more to go,
I feel much better that now you all know.
My grandpa, old and wise.

Stephen Domenichini
Age: 13

MY DAD

My dad is very tall.
He does everything for all.
He doesn't make a fuss.
My dad cares for us!

He has a wife.
The Air Force is his life.
He likes to spend time with us.
My dad cares for us!

My dad is brave.
And gets in trouble if he doesn't shave.
He likes to call us.
My dad cares for us!

Shawn Meczywor
Age: 13

THE BEAUTIFUL SUN

The sun is beautiful,
The sun is bright,
The sun gives everyone
A big shiny light,
The sun is big,
The sun is round,
The sun doesn't give me
A big giant frown.

Davian Madho

DALE EARNHARDT

He was the greatest racecar driver ever
And always did his best
No matter what happened.
He won seven Winston Cup titles
From 1979 through 2001 at the age of fifty.
But he always kept racing and racing.

He never would complain,
Yell, scream, or fight,
He was very intimidating to other drivers
And was never intimidated.
That is why he did so good
And kept racing and racing.

He left four kids and a wife behind
In his crash in the last corner
At Daytona in 2001.
He will be remembered
As the greatest racecar driver ever
Because he kept racing and racing.

Bruce Gaspardi Jr.
Age: 13

ELEANOR ROOSEVELT: ONE OF A KIND

On October 11, 1884 in New York City,
A child was born who wasn't thought of as pretty.
Fearful, shy, and overall plain,
This young girl had a future to gain.
Eleanor Roosevelt, who would have known
That her sensational qualities
Didn't show until she was grown?
Although it took her years to come up from behind,
As an overall person, she was one of a kind.

After three years away to school in London
This young girl did shift
From a young, timid girl into a woman
Who was curious, intelligent, and swift.
Now secretly engaged at only nineteen,
She and Franklin Roosevelt kept the affection
Between them unseen.
Once officially married in 1905,
The two together brought others alive.
Unaware of her future, she kept a firm state of mind.
As an overall person, she was one of a kind.

Now in their twenties with five children of their own,
The couple was becoming very well-known.
At the start of World War I she volunteered at a canteen.
On discovering she enjoyed it so much,
Volunteering became routine.
When Franklin became ill with polio
she acted in his place
To keep the Roosevelt name known
And it worked in this case.
With doing so much and so often
She was a hard person to find.
As an overall person, she was one of a kind.

When her husband became governor she began to teach,
Helping New York City children
Who were sometimes hard to reach.
Then, Franklin was elected President in 1933,
Ready to help the nation,
Whether or not others wanted to agree.
Eleanor Roosevelt, a first lady unlike any other
The nation had seen,
Decided to be herself and not another first lady
Who was quiet and serene.
Helping coal miners, sharecroppers,
And much of mankind,
As an overall person, she was one of a kind.

Whether it was the unemployed, African Americans,
Or others in need,
Eleanor helped countless people
Showing her lack of greed.
Also as a public first lady,
She wrote a column, "New Day".
This was published in papers almost every day.
She was also a leader of women's rights,
And the racial prejudices that often broke out into fights.
She was also Franklin's conscience,
Always there to help remind.
As an overall person, she was one of a kind.

During World War II this first lady went overseas
To help what had happened
Because of the Nazis and the Japanese.
April 12, 1945 her husband, the President,
Mr. Franklin D. Roosevelt slipped away.
Off into the silent, cold, and somber day.
Now on her own, with little to lose,
She was asked to join the United Nations
And didn't refuse.
Now sixty, she still had that original mind.
As an overall person, she was one of a kind.

Eleanor Roosevelt throughout all her years,
Keeping her head held high through laughter and tears.
Helping millions of people, young and old,
Showing her as kind, unselfish and bold.
As America's first lady she displayed courage and hope,
Making it easier for the unemployed, African Americans,
And women to cope.
Considered one of the strongest,
Most giving women of all time,
As an overall person, she was one of a kind.

Kasey Wooten
Age: 14

SOCCER

Soccer is good, soccer is fun.
It is a sport that can be enjoyed by everyone.
Big or small, short or tall,
All you have to know is how to kick the ball.

Halfback, fullback, goalie, or striker,
I don't care what to play
'Cause soccer is fun in everyway.

Courtney Beeman

MOM

My mother
　her life is precious
not only to her but to the beings around her
　to her children
　　husband
　　　siblings
　　　　parents
even the weather loves her
it's like the weather does anything she wants it to.
　She loves life and life loves her
　My mother.

Samuel Blazejewski
Age: 13

WATER

Water runs through the lakes peaceful and clean
Water runs through the waterfall loud as it can be
Water runs through the river crackling away
Water runs through me ninety-five percent of the way.

Alecia J. Detka

TEARS OF STRENGTH

We all remember that horrible, gloomy September day
When everything happened in all the wrong way
Thousands of innocent people died
Millions more watched and cried
We stared at the scene in disbelief and in horror
As the television showed pictures over and over
We waited for the list of who survived
Staring, trying to find out if our loved ones were still
alive
No one will ever forget that September day
When the terrorists struck us in a bad way
But the terrorists failed
They are not going to win by sending anthrax in the mail
We AMERICANS came together
Forever and stronger than ever
We all joined our STURDY hands
To show our STRENGTH for our family,
friends, and land
And united we will always stand.
We AMERICANS will not back away
We got stronger with every dawning day
We will continue to fight
With our might for what is right
We will not lose this war
So let the Red, White, and Blue soar
Let the eagle fly
Into the victorious sky
And don't forget to cry
When you think of the crime
Cry to endless lengths
For those are your tears of strength

Ashley Martin
Age: 13

69

HOW TO BE A FRIEND:

When your world is gray,
When everything is wrong,
I'm here to keep you going
and to keep you strong.

Whenever you're in misery
and have the urge to cry,
Being there and comforting you
is something I'll always try.

Whenever you're in trouble,
When things get out of hand,
come to me, I'll listen
and try to understand.

Whenever you're lost for words
and can't complete a phrase,
I'll lead you out of confusion,
and help you find your way.

When life hands you bitterness,
When people make you feel ignored,
I'll add sweetness to your life
And keep your heart from being bored.

When the sun seems not to shine,
When things become unfair,
I'll be that one to show you
love and care.

You are not just a friend to me.
You are my best friend.
You're someone I can turn to,
count on, depend on.

When I see you sad, with a frown on your face,
I'd rather take over the pain
and hope your pain will erase.

Tianna Fronsman
Age: 13

PATRICIA

Her name was Grandma Pat.
We would sit and read on a mat.
She always had miles of smiles.
She had golden blonde hair with a beautiful flare.
She is always in my heart some way.

We would shop until we dropped.
Vacations were fun too.
Until she got the flu.
Then she was blue.
She is always in my heart some way.

I wish I could fly above the sky.
To see my angel in the sky.
I often cry to see this sight.
But all I can do is say good night.
She is always in my heart some way.

Amanda Alibozek

BREAKAWAY

He passes the defenders
  and gets the ball.
The opponent is coming on fast!

He sprints even faster,
  with the ball at his feet.
A look straight ahead;
  he's excited when he sees the net.

Soon before his eyes
  leaps the goalie.
He holds his breath,
  the kick is his best!
The ball heads for the net...
  SAVED!

The goalie makes the play.
That is the end
  of the breakaway.

Nicholas LeFebvre
Age: 11

EAGLE

Soaring through the sky
how beautiful they fly.
They fly without care of time
one look is worth a whole gold mine.
As long as these birds fly free
Americans will always be free.

Brandon Hoag
Age: 11

ALI

Ali is nice but can be mean.
He is very tough and lean.
He talks a lot and brags indeed.
Ali has a long hard punch and marvelous speed.

Ali weighs in at 178 pounds,
And can make all sorts of sounds.
He is a wealthy man and is not in need.
Ali has a long hard punch and marvelous speed.

Ali is one of the best,
If you want you could put him to the test.
He is a truthful man and keeps a creed.
Ali has a long hard punch and marvelous speed.

Steven Bedard

U. S. A. FLIES

Fly like an eagle,
soaring through the sky,
the U. S. has the freedom,
to live their lives untied.

When we win the final battle,
the mountains, they will sing,
good luck to the U. S. A.,
and let our freedom ring.

Jessica Robinson
Age: 11

MY DOG

My dog is black.
She likes to whack.
Her name is Zacky.
I just call her Blacky.
My dog is always chasing.
Then she comes back racing.
She can be the one,
Then she gets things done.
When she eats a bone,
She makes a weird tone.

Jacob Wilk

NATURE

I look outside my window and guess what I see,
I see the great oak tree.
With its limbs reaching for the sky,
High, high reaching for the sky
Not knowing where it ends.
I look over to my right,
Mother's crying in the night.
Trying to understand my mom's pain,
The light turns to black clouds of rain.
Flowers bloom in the late noon,
Dark skies here comes the full moon.
Rivers flow into distant places,
Still no remembering faces.
Ladies scowl, men shout,
Angry children cry and pout.
As this goes on there's rain then sun,
Springtime has just begun.
You think that people would stop to see,
The wonderful buzz of a bumblebee.
Stars shine bright,
With pure white light,
The time has come to say good night.

Chantal Gates

RAIN

It rhymes with gain, but causes no pain.
It's fun to be out in it, sometimes for an hour,
sometimes for a minute.
The way it makes you feel
is like a chasing a rainbow across a field of dreams.
That's just the way it seems.
Some kids run out to play in the puddles.
SPLASH!!!
Everything in sight is doused in wonderful rainwater.
Flowers, trees, bushes, plants.
Like in a garden, the colorful flowers gleam with
raindrops
sparkling on them from the gorgeous sun.
Now you know why the rain can be so much fun.

Julie Ciskowski
Age: 11

AMERICA

America is my country
where I can roam free.
I will never forget
the tragedy
that happened last year.
Now, makes us all live in fear.
What will happen to this dear country?
America

Samantha Haines

76

MY MOM

My mom teaches me right from wrong
When she works she sometimes sings a little song.
She works with other people and teaches them too.
Teaching preschool is what she likes to do.
With all this work to do,
She still has time to raise five kids and her life to pursue.

She's nice, caring, and sweet as a rose,
To anyone she doesn't have to pose.
She gives me anything I want or need,
I don't even have to plead.
With all this work to do,
She still has time to raise five kids and her life to pursue.

My mom gives me the most love,
And when she hugs it's like a dove.
She's not only a mother, she's also a wife.
She only yells to help us in life.
With all this work to do,
She still has time to raise five kids and a life to pursue.

Kayli Larabee
Age: 14

MY GREAT GRANDMA

Her name was Emma
And Irish she 'twas
I called her "Gigi"
But my great grandma she was

She was always busy cooking
And that is because
She raised seven children
My great grandma she was

You never left hungry
Great food to make us buzz
A warm heart and a big welcome
My great grandma she was

She was a beautiful lady
I miss her because
She passed away last May
My great grandma she was!!

Kelley Burzimati
Age: 13

78

SUCH A DAY

The air is moist,
The sky is gray,
Who'd want to be out
On such a day?

The sky gets dark,
The wind does sway,
Who'd want to be out
On such a day?

The rain does fall,
It's in the way,
Who'd want to be out
On such a day?

The sky gets clear,
It's nice today,
I'd want to be out
On such a day.

Joshua Lyons
Age: 13

79

FRIENDS

Friends are the
Ones who tell
You they care.

Friends are the
Ones who aren't
Afraid to share.

Friends are the
Ones who stand
By your side.

Friends are the
Ones who say
Not to hide.

Please believe me,
I know that
It's true.
I've got great friends.
Do you?

Alison Borey
Age: 11

Nation
Indivisible, free
Caring, aiding, protect
Safe, thankful, proud
U. S. A.

Cody O'Dell
Age: 9

QUINN

Quinn Conally was a great friend,
He always knew what to say, but not at the tragic end.
Quinn was the kind of person who wore a smile,
You could spot it from a mile.
I never got to say good-bye.

Quinn, player on two hockey leagues, youth and travel.
The way he played his game was very inspirational.
He was also very athletic
And he was my role model.
I never got to say good-bye.

December 4, 2000 was the day he died.
When Kyle told me I thought it was a lie.
He never saw the puck fly
On the day he died.
I never got to say good-bye.

Lynsey Betit

U. S. A.
Big, free
Helping, caring, protecting
Glad, safe, peaceful
Country

Tyler Wells
Age: 9

The majestic stallion stands
With his head held high
As if searching
For something in the sky.
His tail waves
Like a flag
Proud and grand
Just like a stag
Ears pricked forward
Heart beating true
Eyes shining toward the sky
That is oh so blue.
His nostrils are flared
Heart brave
Never scared
His legs strong
And not lame
His spirit
Cannot be tamed.

Deena Bak

U. S. A.
Big, free
Helping, aiding, caring
Glad, happy, proud, safe
Land

Richard Aslan Santelli
Age: 9

MOM

My mom is a person who cares,
She is a woman who always shares,
When she works with the sick,
She is the nurse they always pick,
Her favorite thing is to sing.

She cares about others,
Which makes us come together,
She cherishes every moment,
She is clever and very intelligent,
Her favorite thing is to sing.

She's a person full of life,
Not only a mother but a great wife,
She finds time to care for three,
That's a person I want to be,
One last thing, she loves to sing!

Brynne Rivard

America
Brave, strong
Protecting, helping, caring
Safe, thankful, glad, proud
U. S. A.

Leanna Telladira
Age: 8

GARDEN OF LOVE

Garden of love
Is like a sign from up above.
God and His son
Welcome everyone.

God's Heavenly gates are gold
And we are His to hold.
It's better to forgive than hate
That's why the garden of love is great.

We get touched by ANGEL WINGS
That's why love is an important thing.
I used to be a baby now I'm a grown beautiful girl
And I have a mind of my own and I love the world.

Jaimee Elizabeth Collins

A gape with terror,
M any lives taken away,
E ven shedding with tears,
R euniting every day.
I ncident is in the past,
C rying no more.
A beautiful nation, again.

Megan Kolis
Age: 12

DAD

Dad is stronger than a pickle jar
Always gets a par
All the power of a leaf blower
Faster than a speeding lawn mower.

Never does anything wrong
Likes to listen to a song
Not a very good sewer
Faster than a speeding lawn mower.

Likes to walk on ice
Is very nice
He is a very good thrower
Faster than a speeding lawn mower.

Mark Therrien Jr.

A THREE-MILE RACE AROUND THE WORLD

It's the day of the race, there's tension in the air,
After getting off the bus, runners begin to prepare.
Despite the sizzling sun and the blistering heat,
It seems as if everyone is ready to compete.
There's a three-mile race to be run today,
And it will begin very soon without delay.
Way off in the distance a clock counts down,
Until the race will begin with a deafening sound.
As the runners begin their pre-race preparation,
Tensions mount with the growing anticipation.
Each competitor has three things in mind,
The honor, fame, and glory he hopes to find.

Many runners have used their whole summers to train,
They can probably sprint this course without any pain.
You think they will have much too fast of a pace
For you to keep up with them during this race.
Without further ado, they form a horizontal line,
Each runner believing it is his day to shine.
Months of training have come down to this,
An opportunity that no one wants to miss.
Off in the distance, the trees are orange and yellow,
Making the atmosphere somewhat more mellow.
But suddenly with the thunderous blast of a horn,
The three-mile race has been born.

At the beginning of the race the breathing is light,
It is almost as casual as flying a kite.
While the runners trudge along, they keep a steady beat,
As they swing their arms and move their feet.
Before long, a lone runner takes the lead,
He is a lot stronger than the rest of the stampede.
However, when the first mile comes to a close,
He is ahead of you by just a nose.
Just as you begin to think about a winning time,
You see a treacherous mountain that you must climb.
On his face the lead runner must have a smile,
As he doubts that anyone can follow him up a hill so vile.

Nevertheless, you stay with him up the hill,
As you do so, time seems to be standing still.
Then, something happens as you reach the peak.
Suddenly, you do not feel so meek.
You get into a rhythm, some kind of a flow,
During a race that seemed to begin hours ago.
While you hear runners behind you moan,
You have entered into a different zone.
You are unaware that you are in front of the pack,
With many of the runners behind your back.
When the second mile is complete,
You are two-thirds done with the meet.

Unfortunately, this is when you come out of your zone,
You begin to realize that you are not alone.
The last half-mile is the most difficult part,
You wish you could just use a speedy go-cart.
But when you look up, you are amazed by what you see.
The lead runner is not where you thought he would be.
You are surprised that you are so close to him,
That the distance to the front is so very slim.
As the end nears,
Thoughts begin to race through your head.
You might win this race if you can just get ahead.
As you come around the final turn,
In your legs you can feel the burn.

With the finish line beginning to loom close in sight,
You start to sprint with all your might.
The smile disappears from the lead runner's face,
As you take his position in first place.
While the cheers of the crowd
grow stronger and stronger,
Your strides to the finish become longer and longer.
But when the race is over you collapse to the ground,
Unaware of even the slightest sound.
Under the hot sun in a clear blue sky,
The other runners go on by.
Who would have thought before the race did begin,
That you were the one who was going to win.

Thomas M. Koperniak
Age: 17

A CLEVER PORCUPINE

A clever porcupine
standing on its hind legs
early in the afternoon
at the edge of the forest
wandering around hunting for food

Timothy Mesite

HERE COMES THE STORM

Here comes the cloud.
Full of rain like a damp sponge.
Here comes the rain
like God wringing out the sponge.

Here comes lightning
like Heaven's light turning on and off.

Here comes the thunder
like a band of angels playing the drums.

Here comes the storm.

Margaret Murray

HE'S HERE

Brown, gray, green, blue,
yellow, white, I see you.
The monster creeps under your bed,
small black eyes set in his head.
He glares at you for hours and hours,
feels like you're falling from high, high towers.
Shut your eyes, go to sleep.
Here is your nightmare for you to keep.
Call your dad, call your mom.
It won't help, his name is Tom.
Tom the monster is his name.
He will win this scary game.
He wants you to sleep, he wants to take you.
Try not to scream, he'll make you.
He whispers, "I'll get you, I'll get you."
Hiding under your covers won't help you.
Tom the monster under the bed
His words rolling 'round and 'round in your head.
He's got you, he's got you, under the bed.
He'll eat you, he'll eat you from your toes
to your head.

Jessica Garrity
Age: 11

90

Four-wheelers
Honda, Yamaha
Red, green, blue
Fun, dangerous, hobby
Four-wheelers

Matt Degnan
Age: 11

MY DREAM DAY

Wake up really early
Get up the dog
Put the dog in the truck
Go to the duck pond
Load the gun
Stand really still
Wait for the ducks to come
Finally a duck comes
The gun comes to your shoulder
You pull the trigger
You feel the recoil in your shoulder
The duck falls to the water with a splash
Suddenly the quacks fall over the pond
The dog gets excited
You stand really still
Finally the hunt comes to an end
The dog fetches the game

Adam Cooley

THE TIGER AND THE CHILD

Tiger tiger eyes so bright
in the mist of the night
eyes of emeralds a fiery glow
lets all the villagers know,
"I am the huntress and fearless am I"

The tiger growls low and deep,
and out of the bushes she creeps
then suddenly she makes a leap!
the villagers cry
as a small child was taken as hers to keep
"I am the huntress and fearless am I"

And seeking revenge the village men gather
armed appropriately for the matter,
they found the tiger in her den
then there was such a ramble of shots and bangs
until one man shouts, "Stop! She's tame!"
and there stands the child
with a worried look on his face
he stops and kneels on the ground
petting the tiger that is making no sound
in that moment of infamy the majestic tiger ceases to be,
"I am the huntress and fearless am I"

Olivia Sophia Wrobel
Age: 11

THE BEST SIGHT I'VE SEEN

The best sight I have ever seen was the sunset.
It was like an amazing glowing diskette.

It was pink, orange, green, and blue too.
When I saw it, I heard a rooster go cock-a-doodle-doo.

When I saw it I said what a great sight.
I will dream about the sunset all day and all night.

I got a camera and took a picture of that sunset.
I felt so amazed that I saw something so perfect.

I'm so glad that God created a painting like that.
That's a memory I won't soon forget.

If I told my friends and family about this
The colors I describe wouldn't do it justice.

I have my picture now, I can show them all.
And afterwards it will be framed on my wall.

We have these sunsets every night you see.
But this one became very special to me.

I'm thankful for this memory of colors I now have
And even happier
Because it hangs on my wall under glass.

I can call this a painting that God's hand had done
Or a picture I took when the night ate the sun.

Chris Carlson
Age: 12

TUFFY THE CAT

I have a cat named Tuffy,
his fur is soft and fluffy.
He loves to play with a piece of string,
I know in my heart, he will never catch that thing.

We just moved in a brand-new house,
and Tuffy caught his very first mouse.
So beware if you're a mouse or rat,
our house is protected by Tuffy the cat.

Brianna Anderson
Age: 11

QUEEN OF THE NIGHT

Queen of the darkness
Queen of the night
Silver and high in the blackened sky
Encircled by stars
A-winking
A-twinkling
Ruler of the blackness
Ruler of the dark

Until the sunlight blazes through
Cutting like a shark

Cyrena Upham

MY SHADOW AND ME

We dart through the flowers
jump in the earthy leaves
my black twin
just him and me
The sun begins to set
my shadow lengthens into a kingly copy of me
then disappears

Nicholas Paul Lorenzen
Age: 10

AUTUMN LEAF

Autumn has come
Leaves fall
Like the crumbly red one
To the ground
Caught by whispering secrets
Of the wind so high
Down as gracefully as a butterfly
To a flower to get nectar
Now the leaf lay on the soft grass
Captured in the rake
Like a crook in jail
Swept into a pile with other nature friends
For a playful kid to enjoy
Autumn has come

Gina DiTommaso

BACKYARD

Trees circle the lake, surrounding it
The clear blue water shines
Crickets chirp, leaves rustle, a frog croaks
The sun seems to be smiling down on the lake,
Making it glow
In a way that only that lake can

I run my hand down the soft grass
I pick a flower and smell its sweet aroma
The air is crisp and a light breeze blows my hair

The lake is below the cloudless sky
And the sun shines upon it all
An old dead log on its side makes a perfect seat
Though it has lived and died,
It still has a faint smell of pine

The old rock wall sits in the woods
Getting older and older
Some stones out of place,
Lie on the ground
Waiting to be turned over
To reveal the living things
Beneath

A reflection in the lake
The trees admire themselves
As if the lake a mirror

Suddenly a raindrop falls upon the lake
A ripple spreads
Causing the perfect picture to erase

Sounds of rain grow louder
The rain falls harder
Animals scurry into their homes
The trees' branches weigh down with clear liquid
Drops of rain make circles in the water
They spread and the water splashes
As I run home, partially wet.

Alexandra Krasowski
Age: 11

PILLOW WORLD

I went up to a computer to type a letter.
I thought that it might have been better.
When I turned it on something said,
PREPARE FOR TRANSPORT TO PLANET BED.
I got warped to the new place.
I think I got shot through cyberspace!
I met someone at an old willow.
That someone was a fluffy pillow!
I saw the buildings that looked like beds.
I remembered I wanted to be fed!
I went to a pillow restaurant.
What I didn't like was that bed croissant!
I saw a TV which brought me back!
Now I want a really big snack!

Nathan Berry

I LOVE MY GUARDIANS

Looking sleepy they seem alive.
They're my guardians of the bed.
They all stare at me with their big black eyes.
I think they move and come to me.
I feel moved by the way they look.
I have had them all my life!
I love my guardians of the bed!

Sarah E. Lieneck
Age: 10

GONE

You may be gone
But I still remember
The joy I had for you
Going to your camp
Squashing pennies on the railroad track
You may be gone
But I still remember
Your beautiful smile
That I see in my thoughts
You may be gone
But you will always be in my heart
Mary

Shawn Borneman

THE HAWK

Soaring past the river
Searching for a sign,
Diving like a waterfall
Only to fail its difficult test.

Maybe the meadow will be more forgiving,
Providing it with a tasty meal.

Matthew Homer
Age: 10

THE WORN-OUT QUILT

Green and white shapes,
Patterned triangles,
Looking around the room,
Wanting to be held tightly by a child,
Resting sadly at the end of my bed,
Sleepily closing its eyes,
And falling asleep,
Alone with the stuffed animals,
Surrounding it,
It sleeps,
Then suddenly awakens,
From a child holding it,
So happy to be loved,
The worn-out quilt is happy.

Erika Berube

DONKEY

Hairy and fat
And oh, so soft.
It goes, "Hee-haaaaooow!"
Otherwise it's quiet
Until it goes to sleep.
Did I tell you?
It snores so loud!

Donkey

Ryan E. Richard
Age: 8

AUTUMN

The leaves are falling.
The animals are getting food.
Some leaves are red, others are yellow,
Some are even brown.
Autumn is here...
Looking like a rainbow on the ground.
People are raking leaves into piles...
So the kids can play in them.
I collect the colored leaves
To save in my book.

Rachael Sharpe

SUMMER IN MAINE

In summer, the bright sun
Shines over the land
And brings out
The fragrant summer flowers.
Butterflies flutter above the ground
While fish swim in the pond
And crickets sing in the evening.
It's summer in Maine for me!

Lucas LaRoche
Age: 8

HORSE RIDING

H orses are pretty.
O ne is named Black Night.
R iding him is fun to do.
S leeping Beauty is one of my favorites.
E ats sugar cubes.

R iding and practicing at the same time.
I sn't brushing horse hair fun?
D oing things with the horse is fun.
I sn't this horse calm?
N othing can stop me from riding horses or
G oing horseback riding.

Zaquanna Pridgen

WINTER

Winter has come
And brought along
A blanket of sparkling snow.
But it's cold and wet
So I must know:
Why do they call it a "blanket" of snow?

Haley Cwalina
Age: 8

HALLOWEEN

All the costumes and the masks:
  Skeletons,
  Witches,
  Brooms
  And switches,
  Singing stars,
  Cats and horses,
  Princes
  And princesses.
We get dressed up and we get candy:
  Lollipops,
  Caramels,
  Snickers,
  3 Musketeers,
  Milky Ways!

Makayla Dunham

WINTER

You see groups of birds flying south.
You smell snow coming from the sky.
You know winter is here.
You see snowflakes falling from the sky,
Like little pieces of tissue.
It's windy, cold, freezing and crunchy...
A blanket of sparkling snow.
Later, the sky turns so blue.

Eric Cormier
Age: 8

DEVOURER

Take a piece of paper write it up,
Fold it up,
Cut it up.
Over and over 'til there is nothing left except your body
Which is dead because you killed everything.
Now nothing is left.
You killed the trees,
The water,
Other people.
You did it.
You were foolish enough to obey.
You killed everything, even yourself.
Never thinking what you did.

Faith Weis

HALLOWEEN

We decorate the house.
It spooks everybody.
I pretend to be a monster.
I get a lot of candy.
My brother...
Jumps out of the woods...
Says "Boooo!"
And scares me.
I scream!
I love Halloween!

Marleen Bohr
Age: 8

HORSES

Black mane and tail,
Brown fuzzy fur,
Fun to groom,
Hard to braid their mane and tail,
Easy to brush their hooves,
But scary to pick their back hooves,
Always hard to groom
When they are very, very muddy.

Horses

Brittany J. Ovaska

SUN

So, so hot...
You cannot touch it...
Hotter than a volcano...
A star in the middle of our solar system.

Sun

Dylan Bryant
Age: 8

THANKSGIVING DAY

This Thanksgiving we might have family over for a feast.
But we won't eat roast beast.
I usually go over to someone's house
for Thanksgiving day.
Like my memere's.
Maybe we can go to someone's house.
If we play we will have to be as quiet as a mouse.
Give thanks on Thanksgiving day.
Just don't play in hay.
I see and smell the food.
I am in the mood.
I hear lots of people eat.
It has a beat.
We have to go.
We go so slow.
We are happy.

Gabrielle Shantel Turgeon

MY AQUA BIRD

I have an aqua bird
And she has been heard
By my mom, my dad, and me
When she flies around the tree.

Destiny Recor
Age: 8

WINTER

The snow falls down
In small white puffs...
A new season has begun.
Wearing mittens and scarves
We're ready to go
Outside in the snow to have fun.
We'll make a big snowman,
We'll roll the biggest one.
We'll call our mother. She'll say "Oh, my!"
After we are done.
When it's nearly dark
We'll go inside.
When we are through with play.
We'll drink hot chocolate
And climb into bed.
We'll be ready for another day.

Michael Sylvestre

SUNSET

The sunset has many different colors,
And they are loved by my mother.
I love to sit and watch as I admire,
The very pretty light.
I could sit all day and watch it,
The very pretty colors
And the way it is loved by my mother.

Jennifer Lizotte
Age: 11

SIGHTS AND SOUNDS OF THE OCEAN

The Ocean...
I hear lots of sounds
Sea gulls calling
Waves crashing against the wall

The sun is warm
The air is salty
Ships are off in the distance
Blowing their horns

Collecting rocks
Collecting shells
Out on the docks
The ocean I can smell

Morgan Buckley

DOGS

Up and down
  Running all
    around,

Jumping on the couch
  and falling to
    the
      ground,

Getting back up running
  to the door thought
    that it was open,

    Smack
      Smack
        Smack,

  Tried to get up
but all he saw were birds
  flying around his head
then he fell asleep again
    on the ground,
      Hours
        Hours
          Hours

have gone by then he
finally woke up and
he jumped so high
because, a little girl was
looking at him from above.
He ran up the stairs
and hid under his bed.
Then he found his bone
under there and he was
happy again.

Laura Cote
Age: 10

SCARY WITCHES

Pointy hats...
Green mad faces...
Long gray hair...
Ugly black-orange dresses...
Yucky, disgusting fingernails...

Scary Witches

Angel Marie Bourgeois

MONEY

M om said we're too young for money.
O ur mom is just being funny.
N othing can stop us from getting money, right?
E ven though she said that so light.
Y es, it worked, the money is mine, oh yeah!

Demetri Albizu
Age: 9

SUN

The sun is a big flaming ball,
never fail never fall.

The sun is big and round,
every day it warms the ground.

The sun is big and filled with heat,
the sun will never get beat.

The sun is big and filled with strength,
nobody knows the exact length.

The sun is big and will never end,
but this poem must like the rest.

Patrick Schofield

DANCE!

D o you wish you could really dance?
A wonderful place where you can trance.
N obody knows where you are!
C ircling 'round and 'round very far.
I n that dancing mood for a splash
N onstop up on stage,
G iggling I heard from that girl Paige.

Kayla Luoma
Age: 9

MOUNTAINS

They stand high in the sky,
Like a very tall guy

Some for hiking,
Some for skiing

A mountain stands tall to protect us all,
As we feel small

Mountains are all over the world

Mountains are cool

Marty Connors

THE SPORT

What a sport, it is so awesome!
Who doesn't like it?
You should play.
Because it is so easy!
Easy to understand, and easy to enjoy.
If you play it you will like it.
All your friends play, and they say, "Hey!"
"What a sport!"
Hockey.

Shawn Trombley
Age: 11

VIDEO GAMES

Video games are fun to play
Every hour of every day.

I started when I was five.
It is kind of hard to stay alive.

I can beat a level as fast as a fly can fly.
But sometimes I die.

There are so many different things you can do.
My friends like to play them too.

Spencer T. Harrington

HALLOWEEN

Halloween is drawing near,
We listen as the witches start to cheer,
The ghosts and the goblins get ready to scare,
Oh so you better be aware,
The black cats are ready to prowl in the darkness,
The trick-or-treaters are ready for fun,
So you better be ready
Because Halloween is drawing near

Jessica L. Peterson
Age: 10

CLEAN

I went up to my room to play.
It was in May.
I went right in my room
Guess what I saw?

I saw a big huge mess.
I started to put away the huge mess.
I started with my games,
Then I did the cars.

Then I did my bed.
I had old cat food that I fed
To my cat a week ago.
Finally, I finished at seven o'clock at night.

Lisa Dauphinais

ST. NICK'S BIG NIGHT

Sleigh bells are ringing,
He is singing a jolly carol through the night.
Hopping down chimneys of those good kiddies.
He's just a jolly old guy.

Angela Miller
Age: 11

MY HAMSTER'S MISSING

My hamster's missing!
He is out of sight.
Where could he be?
He was gone at night.
So, I couldn't see,
Until it hit daylight.

We looked under beds.
We searched in holes.
Hoping to see something,
But those pesky moles.

We looked at the heaters,
So we decided to check,
And guess what happened.
He popped out his little neck.

Kevin Schuller

A WRITER GREETS A WARRIOR

Walking out upon the battlefield
The only weapon in hand an angry, sharp pen to wield
Ready to raise the tension and be part of the fight
Full of energy uttering a battle cry whether
wrong or right.

The means of attack
The only possible way to fight back
Are through words which into the mind they are lodged
As sharp arrows, and bloody axes are being dodged.

Some fall lying perfectly still on the cold ground
Comprehendible words yet to be found
Others are captured and taken to the opposing side
Their views standing firm as the time they bide.

To some their message is crystal-clear
In others their words instill nothing but fear
Their ideas become thought provoking
As the message to the enemy is life revoking.

The view at hand is stood by until the end
As the enemy makes a mistake no longer able to defend
One side must make a difficult sacrifice
As a sword cuts through the air with a deafening slice.

As the final thoughts are descending
The moment the enemy surely has been dreading
The final punctuation mark ends it all
As the last warrior bravely stands tall.

Lisa Rauhala
Age: 16

115

FLYING AWAY

The young red-tailed hawk
stands on a trainer's hand
in the early afternoon
waiting to fly away.
But will it come back?

Matthew Treen

A DAY AT THE BEACH

I remember...
Sea gulls yelling and calling as they scavenge for food...
The salty sea water rushing onto the beach
As a wave rolls over...
The bitter smell of seaweed as the tide slowly slides out...
The high-pitched squeals and laughter
As children run from a big wave...
The "Slap! Slap! Slap!" of a rock lazily
skipping the water...
Mom yelling, "Time to go!!!" as darkness
starts to creep in...
The sad sound of the car roaring to life
After an exciting day at the beach.

Taylor Andrews
Age: 12

COOL CHRIS

C is for cool brother
H is for helpful
R is for rappin'
I is for intelligent
S is for super
T is for telling the truth
I is for ice-cream eating
A is for awesome
N is for number one

Colin Bradley
Age: 9

AMERICA

A merica is a team,
    Americans have that dream,
M any were lost here,
    Many of them very dear,
E veryone is mad,
…Everyone is sad,
R unning won't help you get away,
…Running gets you in deeper every day,
I wish we could just win this fight,
…I know we will, when the time is just right,
C an we be so giant,
…Can we be so strong,
A merica,
…America, the place where everyone longs.

Haley Andrews

MY LITTLE SISTER GRACE

We give you thanks almighty God, for Grace.
I think she is the best sister in the human race.
She's as smooth as lace and as cool as a pop star.
Grace can be as wild as an animal and also sweet,
But her cry is not neat.
I love my Grace!

Hannah Panteleakis
Age: 8

OLD NORTH CHURCH

O ld North Church is interesting
L ooking at the tall church
D oing a church for a poem

N ature around the church
O ld North Church is tall
R inging a bell
T he Old North Church is along Boston's freedom trail
H ung lanterns there

C ulture built there
H ung lanterns near the church
U nbelievable
R ocks, grass, and flowers are near the church
C hurches are beautiful
H ung lanterns to warn British would attack

Katelyn Daubney

118

STATUE OF LIBERTY

S tatue of Liberty
T his statue is a gift from France
A proud symbol for our country
T ake pride in the statue
Yo U always stand proud
E veryone loves you forever

O n an island in New York Harbor
F ourth of July, 1884 is when you were presented
   as a gift to the United States

L iberty Island is where you stand
I t towers above Liberty Island
   and stands 151 ft 1 inch high
B eautiful and great to have
E nergy is what you need to climb those steps
R ight in New York City
T o be a symbol of freedom
Y ielding hope for those who come to the U. S.

Brittany Furno

MIKE

He's six foot two,
With a size twelve shoe,
And he scares my mother,
For he's a great lurker,
Father, husband, and hard worker.

He loves his children,
And his wife,
And sure enough,
He has a great life,
Father, husband, and hard worker.

He favors his fish,
Makes a wish,
And sees his fantastic job,
And when out on the road he's surely a good parker,
Father, husband, and hard worker.

Two dogs,
Four cats,
And plenty more pets,
He loves the critter,
Father, husband, and hard worker.

He didn't have the chance to go to college,
But still works with many a doctor,
A surgical tech one on one,
With the eyes of all mankind,
Father, husband, and hard worker.

He'd be delighted to meet new people,
And make friends with each and everyone,
He tries to be as polite as possible,
And seizes his opportunities,
Father, husband, and hard worker.

Jonathan Lynn Beals
Age: 13

MY CHICKENS

Rhode Island Red
the very reddest.
Cute and furry
so, so soft.
I love to hold them
in my hands.
Eat their eggs,
they taste so great!
Peck and cluck cluck!
Cock-a-doodle-doo!
Funny noises for me and you.

Sam Robinson

WHAT'S FOR LUNCH?

The cruel leopard
watches carefully
in the midday heat
it walks on the bumpy terrain
stalking his prey.

Andrew Lavin
Age: 10

SUMMER VACATION

S o much fun
U sing new toys
M ore friends to play with
M uch more time to play
E veryone loves to play
R eally fun

V icky to baby-sit
A pples, oranges, and other fruit
C atch the ball
A lways running
T ime flies when you have fun
I am always with a friend
O ften hot days
N ow school is out, time to have fun

Chelsea Rae Grandinetti

MAN OF THE MOUNTAIN

M an on a mountain
A famous rock face on a New Hampshire mountain
N ot a real person

O ut in all kinds of weather
F orever there

T he landmark was discovered in 1821
H ead on the mountain
E dges are sharp all over the place

M any miles in the air
O nly a head on a mountain
U nder the mountain is a road
N ot on a world map
T he rock formation is popular to hikers
A nd may be on a state map
I n the night it doesn't show
N o man carved it!

Bradley LaBonne
Age: 10

PENTAGON

P eople from the Army, Navy, and the Air Force
   work here.
E normous building, shaped like a pentagon.
N ear the Potomac River.
T errorists attacked this building on September 11, 2001.
A merica relies on the Department of Defense.
G uarding our freedom.
O ver twenty-three thousand people work here.
N ear Arlington National Cemetery in Washington, D.C.

Kira Ramirez
Age: 9

GRAND CANYON

G igantic, very steep hill!
R ed rocks covering others.
A rizona is the state I'm found in.
N ot young!
D eveloped by many layers of rock.

C ontinues to grow bigger.
A lways there forever.
N ever leaves its place!
Y our backyard is much smaller than this!
O ne of the most spectacular canyons in the world.
N arrow is right!

Michael Belle

SEPTEMBER

S is for September.
E is for early darkness.
P is for pumpkin pie.
T is for turning leaves.
E is for excitement.
M is for memories.
B is for beauty.
E is for everyone.
R is for rakes.

Nikolaos Panteleakis
Age: 8

PEARL HARBOR

P eople died in Pearl Harbor
E xcellent history sight
A fter they bombed us we went to war
R oar of planes overhead
L ocated on Oahu Island, Hawaii

H ow come they bombed us?
A ttacked by the Japanese
R eaction was shock
B ombs exploding into the night
O ur fleet sunk
R ight and proud America

Nathan Auger - Alves

NEVER FORGET

No matter how hard I try,
           no matter what I do --
               I can't,
                     I just can't --
stop thinking about you.
                    For some reason or another,
                        you aren't like
                           anyone else I know.
When I first met you,
              I don't know exactly why,
                  but I knew that no matter what
                     I wouldn't ever, ever --
stop thinking,
        or forget,
             about you.
                 I wonder sometimes --
if you, like me --
        feel the same
             feelings I get.
                 I wonder...
All I know is that
        I have more
             than just a crush
                on you...

I think that it might be... true love.

                             Emily Owoc
                             Age: 13

STATUE OF LIBERTY

S tatue of Liberty
T he statue stands proudly
A symbol of our country
T all and people depend on it
U sually her torch lights up at night
E veryone looks at it proudly

O ne person designed her
F ire torch

L and stands by her
I t was given to us in 1884 by France
B eautiful statue
E ven some people can't swim to the Statue of Liberty
R ain drops on her
T eachers teach students to build stuff
   and some of those students built her
Y ou don't want to fall off it because it is 151 feet high

James Freeman

It is fading
turning everything
a yellowish orange
as it dies
it darkens the forests
shunning all the creatures
into their homes
it fades the songs
of the birds
as a sparkling blue circle
rises up from the hills
calling out
to the crickets
and the owls
to sing the song
of the night.

Kerstin Sutter
Age: 13

THE THREE ARABIANS

The three brown Arabians,
looking around cautiously,
on a dark night,
in the dry paddock,
listening to the wet whistling wind.

Rachael Rizun

STRENGTH

The strength is in the people who protect us.
Strength was in the Twin Towers.
Strength is in your family.
Strength is in the firemen that save us.
Strength is in our mountains.
Strength is in the birds to fly.
Most of all strength is in your heart.

Nick Harrington

I LOVE YOU

I love, I love
I will love you forever
In my heart I will truly remember
You and all of those who died that September

What you might have seen I will never comprehend
I will never forget you not even in the end
I know that God is loving you
And even from that place above that I cannot explain
I hope you know,
I love you too

Dedicated to Esra

Felicia Scullane

The sky sparkles and twinkles and shines in the sky.
You could make a picture in the sky
And dream up anything you want.
The sky can be so beautiful if you can just look at it.
You can never explain so much beauty.

Maria Canonizado Aglibot

POEM OF PRAISE

Vast things are beautiful:
The waves of an ocean,
The dark solar system,
With planets in motion.
And prairies wide open,
Filled with life,
And castles in England,
With sounds of a fife.

And tiny things are beautiful:
Strands of golden hair,
And ants that scurry and scramble,
In the open air.
Silver beads of a broken necklace,
Shifting through my hand,
And those bluish drops of rain,
Falling on the sand.

Barbara Bemis

EXCUSES

I didn't do it. Did my sister do it?
I don't know who did it.
It wasn't my fault.
Did the dog eat it?
I really don't know who did it.
Was it Mom or Dad?
I am very, very, very confused.
But I didn't. It wasn't me.
I swear it wasn't me at all.
It wasn't me at all. I tell you.
It just happened
All by itself!!

Bobby Croke

INDEPENDENCE

Once we were little
Now we are big

We stand here together
And let freedom ring

We are not afraid
We stand straight and tall

Join hands together
And rejoice with me
The love we have for our country

Victoria Adams

THE NIGHT LIFE

The sun is gone,
The moon is high.
Stars are shining in the vast black sky.
Crickets chirp in the tall, thick grass,
Leading this midnight symphony,
As hours slowly pass.
Fireflies dance upon the cool breeze
Little balls of light flying
Anywhere they please.
Tiny little peeper frogs squeak to one another.
Every now and then you
Hear a faint flutter.
A moth's wings against a window screen.
Bats are flying here and there
Catching mosquitoes everywhere.
An owl hoots and then flies down
To catch a mouse on the ground.
A wolf howls as a sign to all he has begun his prowl.
All is quiet for a mere moment
As old Mr. Possum scampers on by
With an evil gleam in his eye.
Then the air is filled with a strong stench
As a skunk runs under our garden fence.
Suddenly the garbage can makes a loud crash
As a family of raccoons picks through our trash.
Then the sky starts to get bright
with dawn's familiar light
All the creatures return to their homes
To sleep the day away.

Katelyn Beaudoin
Age: 12

I AM SMART AND ATHLETIC

I am smart and athletic
I wonder about my school
I hear chirping and pets talking
I see trees and monsters
I want a PlayStation 2
I am smart and athletic

I pretend to make games
I feel happy
I touch people's hearts
I worry about my family
I cry at times
I am smart and athletic

I understand anything
I say good things
I dream of the future
I try to get high honors
I hope that I will live a Christian life
I am smart and athletic

Jason John
Age: 11

PUPPY LOVE

Puppies are so cute
Yes, puppies tinkle
But my two are the cutest.
They give little winkles. Then
after all, they love me very much.
They kiss me all the time. Yes, they are
mine. You can't steal them or take them.
They're my little buds. So no one can take
them away and our love. Mickey and Mo are
twins, Mo is white, Mickey is black. When it's
time for bed, I say, love ya and good night.

Heather Gove
Age: 11

LIGHTHOUSES

L ight guides ships at night.
I n foggy weather
G lows to help the ships.
H elps boats from crashing.
T here can be a light bulb or a candle.
H ouse for the light keeper.
O ceans made bright.
U sually people go to lighthouses.
S upporting safe boating.
E veryone likes lighthouses.
S een along the coastline.

Nichole Carter

ANIMALS

A nimals, wonderful creatures
N eat
I ntelligent
M oving on the ground
A wesome
L ovable and caring
S pecial

Kristin Roche
Age: 10

WINTER

The sun hides behind the clouds.
The sound of bees is no more.
Then I know it.
Winter is here.
The robins leave.
The days grow cold.
Snow starts to fall.
Then I know it.
Winter is here.
I love winter and fall.
I love spring and summer.
I love them all.
I love winter.

Meaghan Shaw

BETSY ROSS

Betsy Ross created a flag
A beautiful banner in which we brag
A flag flew free
Free, as it should be
A star-spangled banner was born

She made it red, white, and blue
For America to view,
Its beauty waving in the sky
She made it look as if it could fly
A star-spangled banner was born

Washington wanted stripes and stars
Betsy created it carefully
The flag stood true even in wars
They brought it up with a pulley
Atop a pole that stood proud
A star-spangled banner was born

Betsy Ross brought us joy
She brought it to each girl and boy
She is a hero that we praise
And again I will repeat the phrase,
A star-spangled banner was born

Ashli Alberta
Age: 13

MIDNIGHT WALK

Walking on a midnight walk,
I hear some fascinating talk,
from a somewhat lonely man,
talking randomly about a plan.
It was a little weird I must admit,
like an institution where he should submit.
He seemed like he had a caring heart,
but oh so painful like a dart.
Walking on a midnight walk,
I now no longer hear his talk.

Amanda Rabuffo
Age: 13

HOW WE HONOR THE HEROES

Honor all the people who
Who fought in the war

Honor everyone who went
Into the Towers

Honor all the firefighters
That risked their lives

And honor the United States
For being so strong

Chad Sidilau

I AM

I am creative and smart
I wonder about the past
I hear people and animals talking
I want to see the future
I am creative and smart

I pretend I am famous
I feel happy most of the time
I touch hearts
I worry about my family
I cry when someone has died
I am creative and smart

I understand people's conversations
I say good things to someone who is sad
I dream that school will be over forever
I try hard in school
I hope to be successful
I am creative and smart

Rebecca Gazaille
Age: 11

138

MY PERFECT GRANDPA

My family is fun, but my grandpa is special.
He always takes me and my sisters on fun trips
that I wish could last forever.
In early spring we share the joy of gardening together.
He has a tiny bit of gray hair,
and a round head with glasses.
He is my perfect grandpa.
My grandpa has rosy red cheeks and a plump belly,
almost like a beardless Santa.
He has a cute smile
that every now and then I have to giggle at.
He is my perfect grandpa.
When it is time to leave I get the hug I wait for all day.
I love to hear his soft voice say good-bye.
In a flash I miss him but he is still my perfect grandpa.
Sometimes he makes me think.
He is as strong as an ox, and I love him.
Sometimes I want to make a speech
on how lucky I am to have a grandpa like him!

Erin Collins
Age: 8

ONCE UPON A DREAM

Looking up at the ceiling,
I lie in bed.
Just waiting for a candle to light in my head.
Tomorrow I'm speaking to many an ear.
I need to come up with something,
My point must be clear.

People must know what I have seen.
Some of it has been nice,
But most has been mean.
You think we are different,
Our color is to blame.
However on the inside,
We are all the same.
We were created equal to one another.
So why can't you treat us like a sister or brother.

There are these thoughts of mine
That tomorrow must be read.
This is because I know very soon I'll be dead.
How shall I begin about something
Always changing like a stream?
I think I will have it relate to this theme.

The next day I stood up in front of an enormous crowd.
I knew that what I was going to say
Must be said strong and loud.
Stepping forward I thought of life as a stream.
I cleared my throat and started my speech with,
I HAVE A DREAM.

Enrico Palmerino
Age: 14

STARRY NIGHT

I was walking one starry night,
then I saw a beautiful, emotional sight.
In the darkness of the sky,
this creative thing captured my eye.
That night so many things crossed my head,
so many things I could have said.
Swirls and whirls simply amazing,
as I sit there just gazing.
Midnight has now fallen into place
here I still am staring into space.
As I said good-bye, I felt as if I could cry,
I'll see you tomorrow same place, same time.

Kayla Barrows
Age: 12

THE LIGHTHOUSE

Driving by a lighthouse
late on a late summer's afternoon
I'm happy to see the American flag flying high overhead
sun shines brightly over the clear blue Atlantic Ocean
as the flag waves in the breeze.

Megan Menard

I AM WHAT I AM

I am smart and nice.
I wonder about my friends.
I hear a stream flowing and talking pets.
I see deer and unicorns.
I want to have a good life.
I am smart and nice.

I pretend I am a basketball player.
I feel good.
I touch lives.
I worry about family.
I cry when I think about a friend moving away.
I am smart and nice.

I understand animals.
I say lots of things I don't mean.
I dream of friends and animals.
I try my best.
I hope to have a good life.
I am smart and nice.

Krista Nichols
Age: 11

FEELINGS

All people have feelings.
Some people are sensitive, others tough.
Nobody can resist weeping, laughing, or being furious.
Especially when your family or country is hurt badly.

Feelings are a great creation from God.
They are your conscience and your guide.
They express how you are.
They are one of the best creations to have in you.

Let your feelings lead you to forever life.
Don't be afraid to express them.
It shows how attached you are to something.
Feelings are what people need to express themselves.

Timothy Wickstrom Jr.
Age: 10

FEEDING TIME

The mother wolf and her six baby cubs
stare intently at their prey
in the early evening
from their grassy, rocky cave.
It is almost feeding time.

Emily Griffin

FALL

Fall is a time of year
When everything is very dear

People really care today
As the time just ticks away

As leaves fall from the tree
It makes me think of you and me

Anne - Marie Mombourquette
Age: 10

CHEERLEADING

C heerleading
H igh kicks
E very day I listen to the teacher and
E very day I watch TV to learn
R eally pay attention.
L ove to cheer at school
E very day: practice and practice...
A nd it's fun!
D on't forget to bring your pompoms and it's
I mportant to listen in class.
N ever miss a practice.
G ames are fun and cheerleading is too!

Kayla Casalinuova

ONE YEAR LATER

The Twin Towers collapsed in 2001.
September 11 has just begun.
Nothing like this has happened to me.
We all just want to be free.
Those people are gone forever.
This all happened in September.
With new hope we bring some joy,
Which nobody can ever destroy.

Kayleigh Murphy
Age: 9

WHAT IS GRAY

Gray is a touch through an empty room
Gray is black weeping and brown sleeping
Gray is a dark bird crying
Gray is a boring rhyme right off the vine
Gray is a cat covered in soot
Gray is soft whisper in my ear
Gray is a fire when it's dead
Gray is an elephant waking up
Gray is a mouse nibbling on a forgotten soul
Gray is the color of a dark boat
Gray is a tombstone without a name
Gray is the king of all colors

Jacob Goldman

MUHAMMAD ALI

He was a boxer extraordinaire,
When he fought he lost hardly a hair.
Born as Cassius Clay,
He is alive to this day.

Float like a butterfly, sting like a bee,
Who said that? Muhammad Ali.

He was champ in '64,
He never fell to the floor.
He won again in '67,
He didn't want to die in the ring and go to Heaven.

Float like a butterfly, sting like a bee,
Who said that? Muhammad Ali.

He didn't go to Vietnam,
He wouldn't use a gun or bomb.
He retired in '79,
Some say in his prime.

Float like a butterfly, sting like a bee,
Who said that? Muhammad Ali.

Everyone loved the way he fought,
At least that was what he thought.
Now he has a daughter, Liala Ali,
Her father is what she wants to be.
That ends the story about a great,
Where time will determine his fate.

Float like a butterfly, sting like a bee,
Who said that? Muhammad Ali.

Jay Meczywor
Age: 14

SYLVESTER

Sylvester is my pet fish
He lives in a round dish
Around and around he goes by
Making his tail go swish
Always hoping for a bigger dish
Soon, Sylvester will get his wish
Because I just broke his little dish

Danielle Deschene

MY FAMILY

M is for mother.
Y is for I love you.

F is for father.
A is for Andy, my brother.
M is for me.
 I is for ice cream, my favorite food.
L is for love.
Y is for yellow, my favorite color.

Elizabeth Belanger
Age: 9

THE MUNCHIES

The munchies, yes the munchies
Cheetos are like crunchies
These cheesy salty little things
Don't forget the flavor zings
That you get from Starburst chews
They might end up on the news
Don't forget the Ritz Crackers
They might get eaten by the Packers
Everybody likes the munchies
When they're tasty or they're crunchy

Leah Aubin

TREE

Tree, why are you so big?
Tree, why in the fall do your leaves
    change different colors every year?
Tree, why are you green in the spring?
Tree, why do you have leaves?
Tree, why is your stump so brown?
Tree, why does the wind blow your leaves away?
Tree, why do you have to be chopped down?
Tree, why is it in the winter your are bare?
Tree, why do you give homes to animals?

Katelyn M. Graves
Age: 8

MY FAMILY

I love my family very much
I like to keep in touch
I do not mind, because
They are very kind

They do not make me frown
When I am around
Sometimes they will be a pain
But I will always love them the same

Sometimes they make me mad
Other times they make me sad
But they are not that bad
I love my brother, mom, and my dad

Skye Blackmore

THE MUCKY MARSH

Water how did you get so calm?
How did all of the fish and turtles get inside of you?
Dragonfly, how did you get those big wings
to glide over the water?
Grass, how do you get so long?
How did you get here?
Lily pads, how did you get the same name
as our class guinea pig?
How did you get in the water?
Bats how did you fly over the water, why, why, why?
Water spiders, why do you like the water?
Water does it hurt when a bench falls on you,
a frog and turtle goes on you?
Trees does it tickle when squirrels climb up you?

James Toohil Jr.
Age: 8

APPLES

Apples, how did you get green in the beginning?
How did you get so red afterwards?
Do animals nibble at you when you're on your tree?
Does it hurt during the storms?
Who lives in your tree? Birds and squirrels?
Do other animals use you as a home?
What do you see from your home?
What happens after you get rotten?
Do you get eaten?
Apple, oh apple!

Nicole Weldon

TWO BABY SNAPPING TURTLES

Baby snapping turtle how do you swim?
How does your back get so bumpy?
How does your tail get so long?
How is the water? Is it cold?
Is it warm or is it fun?
What do you do underwater?
What do you eat, moss?

Gabrielle Vigeant
Age: 9

NATURE

Hawk, how did your tail get so red?
Bird, how did you get so fast?
Berries how did you get so shiny?
Pond how did you get so wet?
Berries how did you get so red?
Mud you're very black
Rock how did you get so slippery?
Tadpoles how did you turn to frogs?
River how did you get so deep?
Boulder how did you get so big?
Trees how did you get so tall?
Nature how did you get so wide?

Alex Crocker

WHY? MOTHER NATURE

Grass how did you get so green?
How come you're on my TV screen?

Tree how come you're made of bark?
How come you leave a mark?
How come you leave your stump?
I must leave a bump.

Leaves does it hurt when you fall?
How do you ever fall?

Water does it hurt when you freeze?
Does it feel for a nice breeze?

Dirt how come you are brown?
I think you should get a big crown.

Flowers is it great to be pretty?
How come you play with my kitty?

Birds how come you fly?
Mother Nature, Why? Why? Why?

Alexandra Steilen

MOTHER NATURE

Sky how do you get so blue and beautiful?
But then how do you get so gray and gloomy?
Grass how do you get so green and sweet?
But then how do you get so yellow and dead?
Water how do you get so clear and peaceful?
But then how do you get so dried up?
Leaves how do you get so colorful and high?
But then how do you get so brown and shriveled up?
Rock how do you get so warm and smooth?
But then how do you get so cold and wet?
Flower how do you get so tall and bright?
But then how do you get so drooping and dry?
World how do you get so full of amazing things?

Tess Smythe
Age: 8

THE POND

Pond how do you get so wet?
Is it OK if we swim in you?
Do you like it when you are muddy all the time?
Pond do you cry when we throw sticks at you?
Is it OK if flowers grow in you and bugs walk on you?
Pond, I didn't want to leave
but now I have to say good-bye.

Haley Vaudreuil

The leaves are different colors.
The wind feels nice.
The helicopters are big.
They fly just above the trees.
The land is a nice place to be.
School is fun!

Brandon Saucier
Age: 8

SILENCE AND SCREAMS

Although people are silent
when they're being teased
and tormented, I and many others
can hear their screams inside
As they suffer in silence
ready to fall apart
We can bring them back
strong and sturdy with respect
Respect their things
and respect their feelings
Most of all, so we can stop wars,
end hatred towards each other
and bring peace and happiness
back to life in school, in our
hearts and most of all in the world
So there will not be any more
silence and screams

Nora Anderson

BABY SNAPPING TURTLE

Baby snapping turtle, why do you sit on logs?
Baby snapper why can't I find you?
Baby snapper, what do you eat?
What is your name?
Is it David, or Davis, or Louis, or Joe, or even Devon?

Devon Archambault
Age: 8

CAT CRAZE

I'm crazy about cats!
You know it too.
I love white cats, gray cats, and black cats too.
I love calicos and tabbies, I want them all!!!
I'm crazy about cats as you can see.
If I could be an animal a cat it would be!
I want another cat. They would be up to my knee!!
I love my cats.
I love them all.
If you have a cat for sale give me a call.
I'm crazy about cats, yes, I am.
I don't care what people say.
I'm proud of it too!

Theresa Giardini

MY TWO BEST FRIENDS

Mother Nature why are you so cruel? Are you?
Why did you let my two true friends die? Why?
They were! Why did you let them die?
WHY! WHY!
I wish they were still here!

Zoë Kintzer
Age: 8

FALL FUN

I love the fall.
It is the best time of all.
I get up from bed,
And look in the shed.
I grab the rake,
While my mom starts to bake.
I go in the house,
As quiet as a mouse.
I'll run and play,
And skip all day in the merriest way.
In the fall,
The best time of all.

Corinne Kennedy
Age: 9

BIRDS

Birds, birds, do you get smushed in that birdhouse?
Birds, is it fun to fly or is it scary?
Can you see things better?
Does it hurt your voice when you go caw?
Birds, does it hurt when you lay your eggs
or when you make your nest?
Does it hurt birds?
Is the water good?
Is the worm tasty?
Bird, what do you name your babies?
Bird, does it annoy you when the winds blow
or do you like it?
Birds? Birds?

Brianna King

PEOPLE

Why are people different? Why not the same?
Why are people boys and girls?
Why not all girls or all boys?
Why do people have to start out as children?
Why not just start out as grownups and then be children?

Sarah Hookailo
Age: 8

A NEW, HAPPY DAY FOR ELMO!

It's a new day Elmo says as he wakes up with happiness
He's ready to make someone's day the best it can be
He puts a smile on their face -- he does this the best
He's warm, fun, and snuggly as we all can see!

Elmo lights up the screen along with his happy scene
Every time he appears Elmo excites everyone!
Even the TV dances when Elmo appears on the screen.
If you're not smiling his job isn't done.

A new toy is created in Elmo's land
One that will be a very big hit
It tickles, it laughs, and it smiles
This toy is sure to be high in demand!
Elmo's excitement even makes the toys come alive.

Elmo is the one that everyone loves
He always gives one hundred percent --
No more and no less
He even sleeps with a smile on his face. Until...
It's a new day Elmo says as he wakes up with happiness

Jessica Eidinger
Age: 13

158

MY DAD

My dad is the king in my world
And I am his little girl.

We go to the amusement park
And he holds me when it's dark.

I would never trade for a new dad
Because he's not that bad.

We go everywhere together
And there is nobody better.

When I go to bed,
He kisses me on the head.

My dad is always there when I cry
And I will be there when he dies.

Elizabeth A. Mihalak
Age: 11

I CRIED SO HARD

I cried so hard June 21st
I thought my tears would flood the earth

As I shook Mr. Keating's hand he said,
"Be good next year"
"I will," I said

"Thank you for that note," Mrs. Fahey said
"No problem," as I moved ahead

"Thanks for a great year," Mr. Farren said
"No, thank you," I said

"You kept me running some days Jenna,"
as I hugged Mrs. Mason
This was it I could feel it coming

I put my hand out to shake his hand
"Oh no, I've been with you for two years,
I'm giving you a hug," Mr. Tremblay said

Then it happened I cried so hard I could not see
Even the people standing next to me

I dried my tears and went to Mr. D
"I'm on your team," I said

"All right!" he yelled as he gave me a high-five
Then I turned away and started to cry

I cried so hard I could not see
And Evan and Kyle tried to comfort me

"Don't cry it will be okay
Just pretend like it's any other day"

Kyle took my hand as I walked away
And gave me a hug and told me it would be okay

I cried so hard I could not see
Then I realized, I had to go to Mr. Cullen's team

I dried my eyes once again
And told myself don't cry in front of him

There he was sitting on a group of desks
He turned and looked, "I'm not on your team," I said

"Oh, well that's okay, you have Mr. D"
I turned and looked away

"What are you not okay with that?" he said
"No I'm fine with that,
I just had to say good-bye to my teachers," I said

I cried so hard I could not see
"Don't worry, it'll be okay,
you'll be able to see them again," he assured me

"I know but it's not the same"
And I turned and walked away

I cried so hard I could not see
I wondered, "Why is this happening to me?"

I love my teachers with all my heart
Now it hurts to say we're apart

Jenna Cappucci
Age: 13

DESSERTS

Every dessert is awesome
Some Jell-O to pecan pie
I love chocolate chip cookies
And ice cream piled high
        high
        high
        high

Some of my favorite desserts are
Fudge brownies and cake
Mud pies cookies and tarts
Boy those are fun to make

Doughnuts for breakfast
Chocolate pudding for lunch
Apple pie for supper
I love desserts a whole bunch

Emily Biegner
Age: 10

PEACE: WHAT IS IT?

What is peace? I'm asked a lot,
Some say it's full of luck.
Some people say it's a wonderful gift,
But on September 11, it was missed.

Sometimes people look back on that day,
And ask back in time,
"Where was God today?"
But God was with us all the way.

From the Towers to Washington, DC,
And in Pennsylvania people had to see.
The destruction that went on,
It wasn't meant to be.

Just like Pearl Harbor,
But in modern time.
This day will live in infamy,
It was an awful crime.

September 11 was a miserable day,
It was work and rescuing, not play.
But who could forget the awful event,
When America was stuck in a net.

After the 11th it seems to me,
There are more flags and symbols.
People seem more united.

But that's not the point,
It shouldn't have happened.

Michael W. Lefebvre
Age: 11

THE WISE ONE

I am The Wise One.
containing wisdom from my roots to my leaves.
I am The Wise One.
I have been living for many many centuries.
Every ring in my trunk contains a year of children
running, playing within my old old branches,
contains the sight of one last leaf
falling slowly to the ground.
But I have seen so many sorrows
and for them I cry without a sound.
And yet with all this wisdom someone decides
to cut me down, with one last chop to end me.
But come and count my years of life,
for I am passing this to you,
all my memories, happiness, and strife.
For I am The Wise One, I am a tree.

Charlotte Koch

SPECIAL PLACE

Beach under twilight
skies.
Crabs across the
shoreline.

Sea gulls looking for
hidden meals.
Waves breaking across
the water.

Mussels and clams
hiding from prey
hoping people will
scare them away.

Dim light shows
beyond the distance
as the sun sets
this minute.

Barnacles lying on
a rock
living peacefully.

I can hear in the distance
homeless people playing music
for money.

As giant waves break
over the beach,
we leave for now and come back
next week.

Tucker Moore
Age: 10

WIND

When the wind is playful it twines around each leaf
  and stretches across from limb to limb.
When the wind is angry it raises storms from sin.
When the wind is peaceful it lets out a mysterious,
  misty sigh across the peaceful sky.
When the wind is tired it sings a lullaby.

Kathleen Dreher
Age: 10

TOO LATE

Copper was outside in the winter
I felt bad
I asked if he could come in.
Mom said I could
I went outside up to the pen
Yelling, "Copper! Copper!"
As he ran to the gate door
The dog licked my hands
Through the metal gate.
I unlatched the pen door.
Copper jumped out from the door
So happy to be let out of that pen.
I brought him inside.
After fifteen minutes
I let Copper get a drink in the garage.
He went to a bucket
That what I could see looked like water.

In the morning I woke up
Copper was acting weird
Like he was drunk
My parents yelled
"STAY BACK"
My dad rushed Copper to the vet
He called from the vet
But it was too late.
Copper was going to get put to sleep.
We cried
For he was a young dog.
The I said he was drinking from a bucket
We went to look in the bucket.
In it was antifreeze.
It was too late.

Candice Cormier
Age: 11

IT'S FALLIN' IN NEW YORK

In the New York streets of my town,
The leaves are fallin' to the ground.
In so many colors, red, yellow, and brown.
So high, above my head, the sky is full with leaves.
I run to catch 'em but they fly away,
They fly away throughout the day,

Out of the busy streets in New York.
They fall down to the ground,
For the end of that day.
Wow, what a busy day.
They sleep silently in the night,
When the moon is bright.
When the first light hits New York alleys, they lift,
Waiting for the first blow of the wind,
Off again, out of the city.
The wind never letting a child grab hold,
For those leaves are made out of gold.

Elena Rogers
Age: 10

BOSTON BAKED BEANS

boiling baking in a big iron pot
coiled in syrup steaming hot
sweet as a treat cooking all night
over the fire with the stream rising
    higher
  and
higher
for the Sunday meal

Heather Fisher
Age: 10

9/11

The pilots took their final flight
The firemen fought their final fight
The workers had their final night
The day was wrong and never right
Full of fear and fire and fright
The day that seemed to have no light
Like a rope pulled taut and tight
And then it all went white...
   The Towers had fallen

Cristianna Marks
Age: 10

HEAVEN

Above the birds and bees,
Above the earth and trees.
Way up high
In the sky
People fly.
They dance,
They smile,
All the while,
Looking down at you.
And remember the life they had.
Never missing a moment,
Never missing a breath you take,
They are there for you.

Ashleigh Welch